A FIRST LOOK AT AMERICA'S PRESIDENTS

GROVER CLEVELAND

The 22nd & 24th President

by K.C. Kelley

Consultants:
Philip Nash, Associate Professor of History
Pennsylvania State University
Sharon, Pennsylvania

Soo Chun Lu, Associate Professor of History
Indiana University of Pennsylvania
Indiana, Pennsylvania

BEARPORT PUBLISHING

New York, New York

Credits

Cover, Courtesy White House; 4, Courtesy Cornell University Library; 5, Courtesy National Archives; 6, Courtesy National Park Service; 7T, © Glasshouse Images/Alamy; 7B, © North Wind Picture Archive/Alamy; 8, © Iakov Filimonov/Dreamstime; 9T, © Andrey Eremin/Dreamstime; 9B, © Kewuwu/Dreamstime; 10, Courtesy Library of Congress; 11T, © Aivolie/Dreamstime; 11B, © Paris Pierce/Alamy; 12, © North Wind Picture Archives/Alamy; 13T, © Ongchangwei/Dreamstime; 13B, © North Wind Picture Archive/Alamy; 14, Courtesy National Portrait Gallery; 15T, © Vacclav/Dreamstime; 15B, Courtesy Wikimedia, painting by Anders Zorn; 16, © Photograph by Evi Numen. The image is used by kind permission of The College of Physicians of Philadelphia; 17, © North Wind Picture Archives/Alamy; 18, © Peter Spirer/DT; 19T, Courtesy Wikimedia; 19BL, © Paul Lemke/Dreamstime; 19BR, Courtesy White House; 20T, Courtesy National Park Service; 20B, Iakov Filiminov/Dreamstime; 21T, © Paris Pierce/Alamy; 21B, © North Wind Picture Archive/Alamy; 22, © Franck Photos/Alamy; 23T, Courtesy Library of Congress; 23B, © Andrey Eremin/Dreamstime.

Publisher: Kenn Goin
Editor: Jessica Rudolph
Creative Director: Spencer Brinker
Production and Photo Research: Shoreline Publishing Group LLC

Library of Congress Cataloging-in-Publication Data

Names: Kelley, K. C., author.
Title: Grover Cleveland : the 22nd and 24th President / by K.C. Kelley ;
    consultant, Philip Nash, Associate Professor of History, Pennsylvania
    State University.
Description: New York, New York : Bearport Publishing, [2017] | Series: A
    first look at America's presidents | Includes bibliographical references
    and index. | Audience: Ages 4–6.
Identifiers: LCCN 2016020807 (print) | LCCN 2016020909 (ebook) | ISBN
    9781944102678 (library binding) | ISBN 9781944997328 (ebook)
Subjects: LCSH: Cleveland, Grover, 1837–1908—Juvenile literature. |
    Presidents—United States—Biography—Juvenile literature.
Classification: LCC E697 .K44 2017 (print) | LCC E697 (ebook) | DDC
    973.8/5092 [B] —dc23
LC record available at https://lccn.loc.gov/2016020807

For more information, write to Bearport Publishing Company, Inc., 45 West 21st Street, Suite 3B, New York, New York 10010. Printed in the United States of America.

10 9 8 7 6 5 4 3 2 1

CONTENTS

An Honest Man 4

Working Hard 6

A Leader in Buffalo 8

The Governor 10

Helping the Nation 12

A Big Loss 14

A Tough Term 16

Remembering Cleveland 18

Timeline 20

Facts and Quotes 22

Glossary 23

Index 24

Read More 24

Learn More Online 24

About the Author 24

An Honest Man

Grover Cleveland is known for serving two **nonconsecutive** terms as president. He's also known for being an honest man who worked hard to help the American people.

Cleveland ran for president in 1892, with Adlai Stevenson (right) as his vice president.

One term as president is four years. Grover Cleveland was president from 1885 to 1889 and again from 1893 to 1897.

5

Working Hard

Stephen Grover Cleveland was born in New Jersey in 1837. He was the fifth of nine children. His father was the minister of a church. After his father died in 1853, Stephen worked to support his family.

This was the Cleveland's home in New Jersey. The family moved to Fayetteville, New York, when Stephen was four years old.

Cleveland was called Stephen as a child. When he grew up, people began calling him by his middle name, Grover.

Stephen worked in a store like this one when he was 16 years old.

When he was 17, Stephen worked as an assistant to his brother who was the principal of a school in New York City.

A Leader in Buffalo

When he was 18, Cleveland moved to Buffalo, New York, and studied to become a lawyer.

In 1870, he was elected county **sheriff**. Cleveland was good at his job. In 1881, voters elected him mayor of Buffalo!

Cleveland worked long hours as a lawyer.

As sheriff, Cleveland was in charge of the prisoners in the local jail.

SHERIFF

In the 1880s, many people in Buffalo got sick from drinking unclean water. Mayor Cleveland had a new, safer water system built.

After only a year as mayor, Cleveland was elected **governor** of New York. He signed laws to protect areas of nature. He also blocked laws that wasted public money. The American people saw he was a good leader. In 1884, Cleveland ran for president and won!

In the late 1800s, many children worked long hours in factories. Governor Cleveland signed laws that limited child labor in New York.

As governor, Cleveland helped protect areas of New York such as Niagara Falls.

Cleveland ran for president in 1884, with Thomas Hendricks (right) as vice president.

OUR COUNTRY'S CHOICE

DEMOCRATIC NOMINEES

11

Helping the Nation

President Cleveland was a fair leader. Some politicians wanted to hire their friends for government jobs. However, Cleveland hired only people who were honest and would do a good job.

Cleveland

Cleveland hired honest men like himself to help him run the country.

In the late 1800s, farmers used trains to transport their crops to markets across the country. Cleveland worked to make sure train companies did not charge farmers too much money.

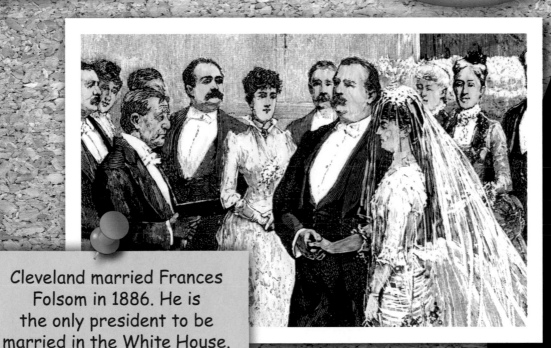

Cleveland married Frances Folsom in 1886. He is the only president to be married in the White House.

A Big Loss

Cleveland worked hard to help Americans. Yet he knew he could do a lot more. So in 1888, he ran for another term as president. He ran against Benjamin Harrison. It was a close race, but Cleveland lost.

Benjamin Harrison

When the Clevelands moved out of the White House, Frances predicted she and her husband would return in four years.

Frances Cleveland

15

A Tough Term

Frances Cleveland was right! In 1892, her husband ran for president again and won. His second term was more challenging. In 1893, trouble hit the nation's businesses. Millions of workers lost their jobs. Other workers went on **strike** because of poor working conditions. Cleveland sent the army to Chicago to end a strike.

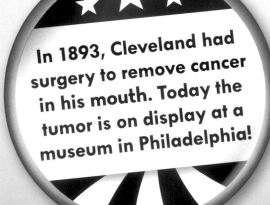

In 1893, Cleveland had surgery to remove cancer in his mouth. Today the tumor is on display at a museum in Philadelphia!

Workers at a Chicago factory that made railroad cars went on strike in 1894. Cleveland sent troops to end the strike.

Army troops

17

Remembering Cleveland

After his second term as president ended, Cleveland moved to Princeton, New Jersey. He worked at the university there. Cleveland died in 1908. Today he is remembered as a president who worked hard to do what was right.

Princeton University

Buffalo remembered its former mayor by naming a high school after Grover Cleveland.

Parts of the Adirondack Mountains in New York are protected thanks to Cleveland.

19

TIMELINE

Here are some major events from Grover Cleveland's life.

1837
Stephen Grover Cleveland is born in Caldwell, New Jersey.

1870
Cleveland is elected sheriff of Erie County, New York.

1840 1850 1860 1870

1841
Cleveland's family moves to Fayetteville, New York.

1859
Cleveland becomes a lawyer in Buffalo, New York.

1882

Cleveland is elected governor of New York.

1884

Cleveland is elected president.

1908

Cleveland dies in Princeton, New Jersey.

1880

1886

Cleveland marries Frances Folsom.

1892

Cleveland is elected president for a second term.

1890

1900

1910

1881

Cleveland is elected mayor of Buffalo.

"I have tried so hard to do right."

One of Cleveland's nicknames was "Grover the Good."

In 1895, Cleveland became the first president to be filmed with a movie camera.

Cleveland loved baseball. In 1885, he invited the Chicago White Stockings to visit the White House.

The Baby Ruth candy bar was named after Cleveland's daughter Ruth.

"Honor lies in honest toil [work]."

22

GLOSSARY

child labor (CHILD LAY-bur) young children working at jobs, often for long hours in unsafe conditions

governor (GUV-ur-nur) the leader of a state

nonconsecutive (*non*-kuhn-SEK-yuh-tiv) not in a row; not back-to-back

sheriff (SHARE-if) the person in charge of enforcing the laws in a county

strike (STRIKE) an event in which people refuse to work until pay or other conditions are agreed upon

tumor (TOO-mur) an unusual lump, which is sometimes cancerous, inside the body

Index

Adirondack Mountains 19
Buffalo, New York 8–9, 19, 20–21
Chicago, Illinois 16–17
childhood 6–7
child labor 10
Fayetteville, New York 6, 20
Folsom (Cleveland), Frances 13, 15, 21
governor 10–11, 21
Harrison, Benjamin 14
Hendricks, Thomas 11
New Jersey 6, 18, 20–21
New York City 7
Niagara Falls 11
Princeton University 18
Stevenson, Adlai 4
strike 16–17
terms as president 4–5, 14, 16, 21
tumor 16
White House 13, 15, 22

Read More

Gaines, Ann Graham. *Grover Cleveland (Presidents of the U.S.A.).* Mankato, MN: Child's World (2008).

Stabler, David. *Kid Presidents: True Tales of Childhood from America's Presidents.* Philadelphia: Quirk Books (2014).

Venezia, Mike. *Grover Cleveland: Twenty-Second and Twenty-Fourth President.* New York: Children's Press (2006).

Learn More Online

To learn more about Grover Cleveland, visit
www.bearportpublishing.com/AmericasPresidents

About the Author:
K.C. Kelley has written many biographies for young readers, including books about Betsy Ross, the Wright Brothers, and Milton Hershey.